Carving Wooden Critters

by

Diane Ernst

To order a copy of this book,
please send cover price plus $2.50 to:

Fox Chapel Publishing
Box 7948 J
Lancaster PA 17604

Please try your favorite book supplier first!

Table of Contents

Foreword

The patterns and instructions in this book are for use by carvers of all levels of skill.

When I carve, I use a Foredom® flexible shaft power tool from start to finish, so my comments and suggestions will be referring to this method of carving. Of course, these ideas may be applied to any method of carving you choose.

The wood I prefer is Basswood. Its clean, white color and lack of grain make it ideal, in my opinion, for this type of work. I also like the way it takes wood burning.

Most of the carvings shown in this book are finished with wood burning. I don't usually do anything else to the piece because this is the way I like my carvings to look. However, I would encourage you to experiment with paints and other types of finishes to see what you like best.

When I set out to draw a pattern, one of my goals is *not* to attain photographic realism, but to bring out the charm and character of the subject. I want my carvings to grab the eye and create the urge to touch. I believe that 90 percent of the character is found (or lost) in a carving's facial expression. On one occasion at a carving show, a gentleman picked up one of my bears to get a better look. "When you look at his face, you get a surprise," he said. Then he bought it!

As you start to carve, the most important goal you should have is to *please yourself!* With that in mind, let's see how you do.

Techniques and Tools

1 Mark a blank with pencil to show where and how to start shaping.

2 Mark these guidelines on the back of the blank as well.

3 Use a large cone-shaped burr to shape the bunny. Be sure to turn and work all sides of the bunny.

4 Reapply the pencil marks for the eyes, nose and mouth as you carve. You'll find that placement of the facial features is easier this way.

5 When your carving looks like this, change to a smaller, tapered burr. Use a spherical burr to hollow the ears.

6

A back view of the roughly shaped bunny.

7 With the tapered burr, cut in the outline of your bunny's eyes, nose, mouth and limbs. Don't be afraid to cut fairly deep.

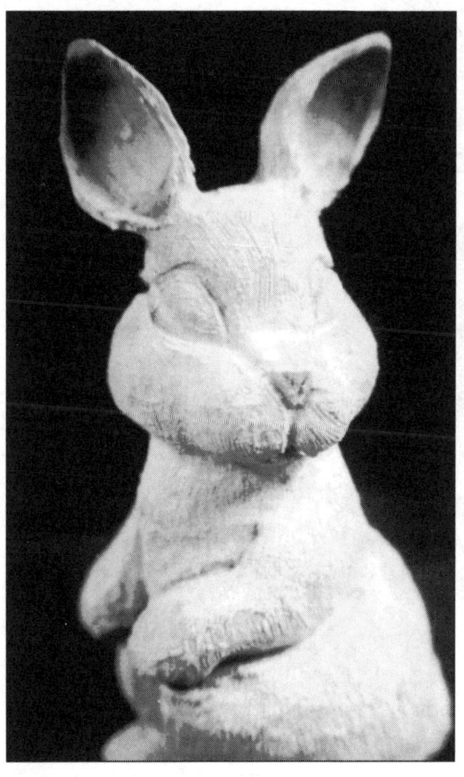

8 Still using the small burr, round off the edges of your outlines.

9 Now begin sanding. Use a sanding drum with 220 grit paper. Carefully sand away all burr marks. In places where your drum doesn't fit, use a skinny mandrel with 220 grit. Pencil the details in again.

10 Using a tear-shaped diamond cutter, cut in outlines for eyes, nose, mouth and limbs as you did before. This time, show a separation between the eyeballs and eyelids. Using the same cutter, refine these details carefully. Keep checking for balance in eyes.

11 Change to a needle-shaped diamond cutter. Use this cutter to sharpen eyelids and nostrils, and to indicate toes. Use a cylinder-shaped diamond cutter to texture the tail. Hold the cutter at an angle so only the edge touches. Clean up the "fuzz" with sandpaper.

12 Time to do the final sanding. Start with the mandrel to remove any remaining tool marks, then switch to hand-held 220 grit paper. Sanding takes time! Continue to sand until the wood is smooth all over. The better you sand, the better your burning will come out later.

13 Pencil in the fur pattern. Pay attention to the direction in which the fur lies; it follows the curves of the body. A dog or a cat is a good example. Mark dark and light areas, as well as direction.

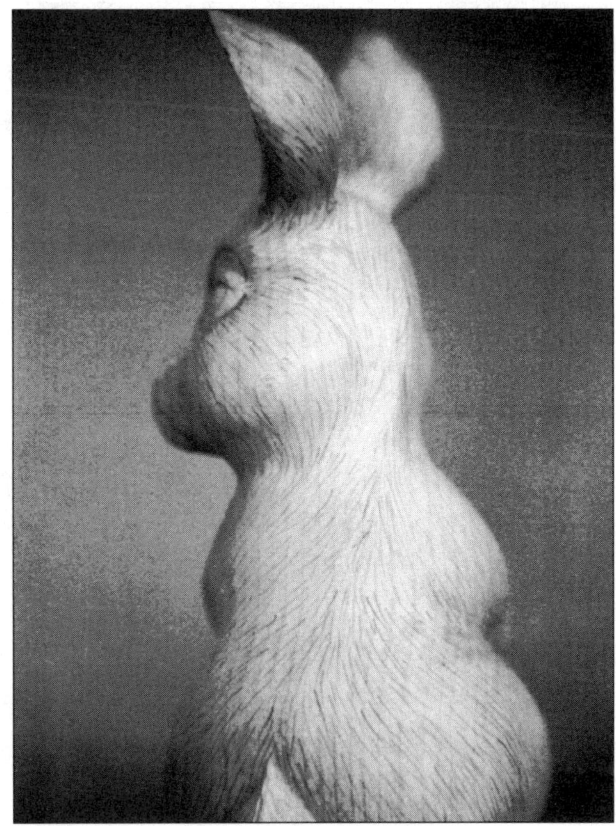

14 This view of the bunny shows the fur pattern on the bunny's back.

15 Start burning the nose and eyes by laying the burner point flat on the surface of the wood. Slide it carefully over the wood, creating a shiny, leathery feeling. Keep the tool moving to avoid flat marks. Start burning on the fur at the nose using short straight strokes. As you work toward areas where the fur is longer, use longer, curved strokes. Leave the light areas for later.

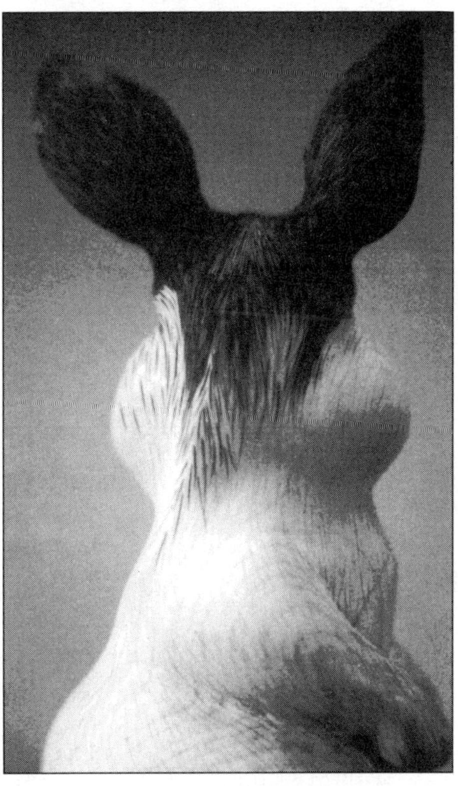

16 The burn marks on the back of the bunny's head will look like this.

17 Continue on this way following your guidelines until the dark fur areas are filled in.

18 Turn down the setting on your burner and, with a very light touch, fill in the light areas. To burn the tail, use a low setting and the same techniques you used in Step 15. Nice job!

Finishing Tips

PANDA

To give the panda its fur texture, I start with a cylinder-shaped diamond cutter and go over the entire animal, following my penciled guidelines. I clean up the "fuzz" with creased sandpaper or an old tooth brush. Then I wood burn the black areas with the wood burner set fairly high. The white areas will be more of a vanilla-white color, but I prefer this look to a painted one.

HARP SEAL

When I do carvings of sea creatures, I like to use butternut wood because of its beautiful grain. For the best results, I take special care to sand the surfaces very smooth, removing *all* tool marks. I use high gloss tung oil to finish this type of carving. It is best applied with a soft cloth. I use a small brush for harder to reach spots. After each coat of oil dries, I rub it down with very fine steel wool before applying the next coat. I'm usually satisfied with the shine after the fourth coat. I DO NOT steel wool after the last coat of tung oil.

PUPPIES

The puppies can be finished any number of ways. The ones pictured in this book were painted with acrylics. Wonderful effects can also be achieved through the use of stains. To create spotted puppies, use a dark stain for the spots and finish the piece with tung oil. A good stain will allow the wood's grain to show through.

ORNAMENTS

When carving these ornaments you can make them as plain or elaborate as you choose. They can be finished with stain or paints. To make a painted "flat," just cut out the shape from 1/4" or 1/8" wide wood, then sand and paint. Finish with varathane. For a more "crafted look," use 1" wide wood and carve "in the round," as you would a large carving. I then paint carefully and rub with steel wool for an aged effect. The rocking horse shown in this book was carved in the round with two separate rockers, painted with bright acrylic colors, and finished with varathane.

Tools

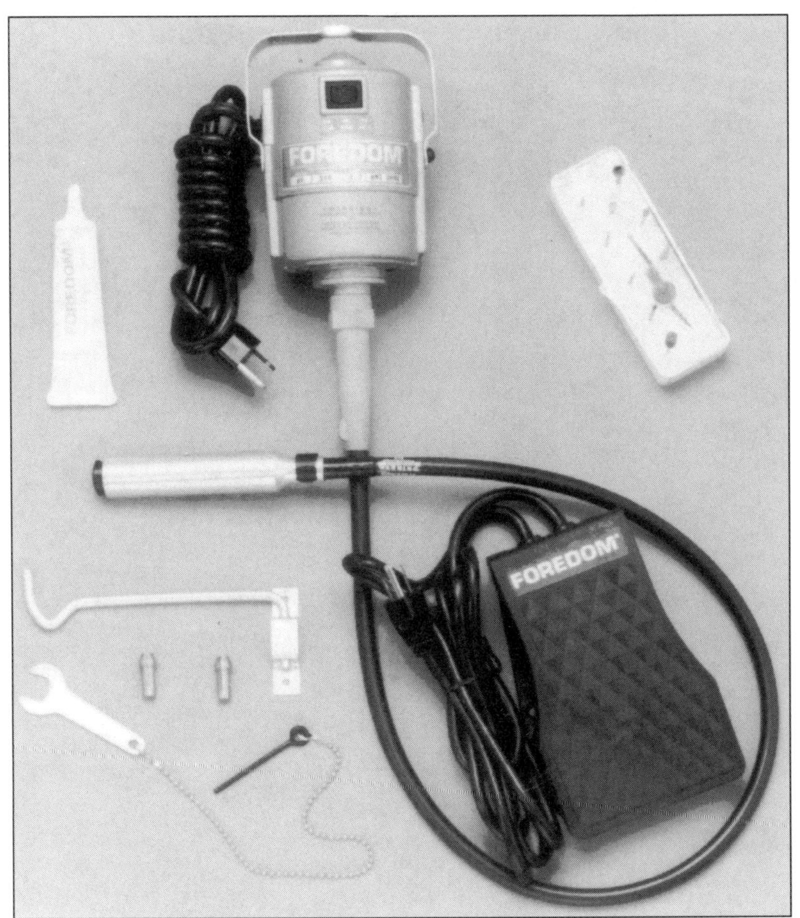

The Foredom Model 5240 Reversible is a popular flexible shaft machine for power carvers.

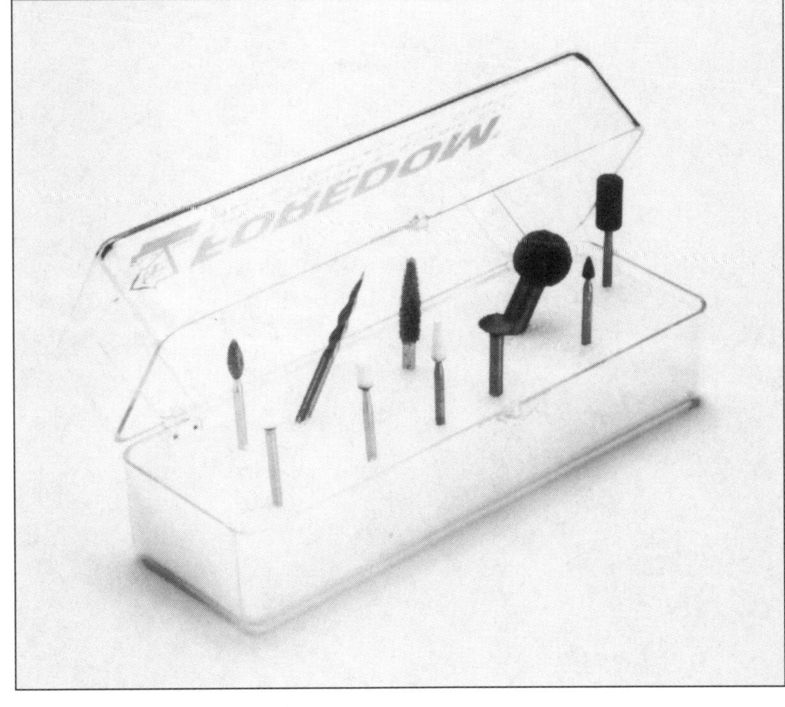

A selection of popular burrs and tips for the power carver. Back Row: Tear-shaped, carving twist drill, cone-shaped, ruby spherical burr, vanadium steel cutter. Front Row: Three aluminum oxide points used for fine detailing, two red oxide points.

Patterns

Bunny Pattern

Taking a Break

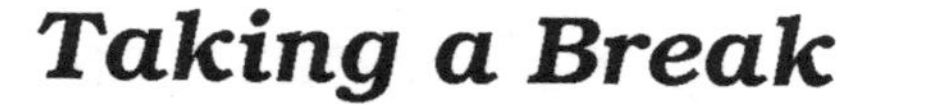

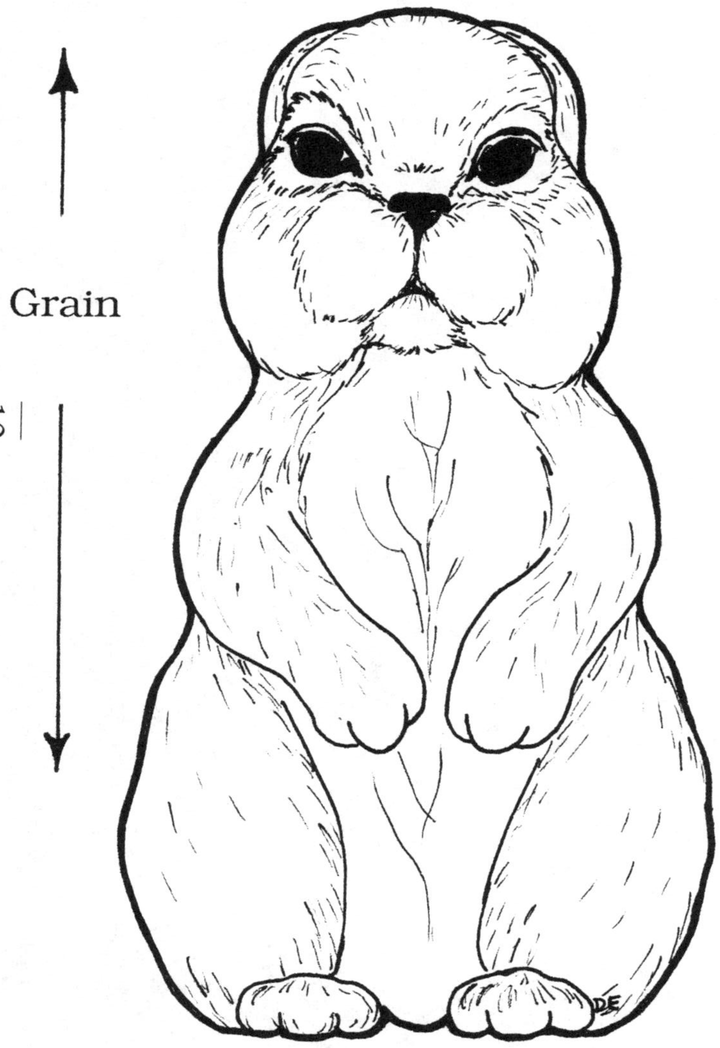

Front

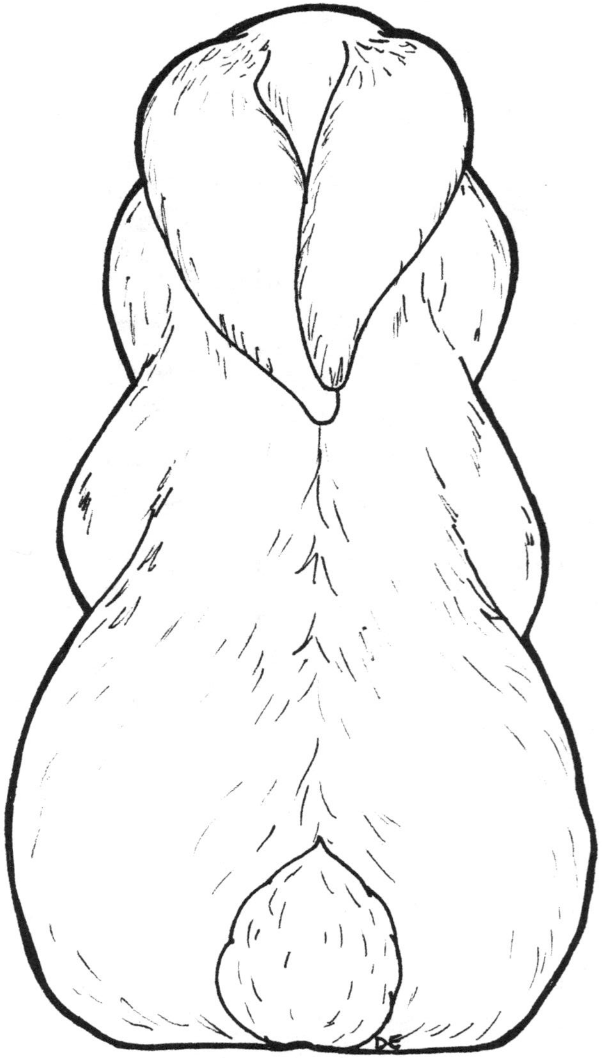

Back

Bunny Pattern

Taking a Break

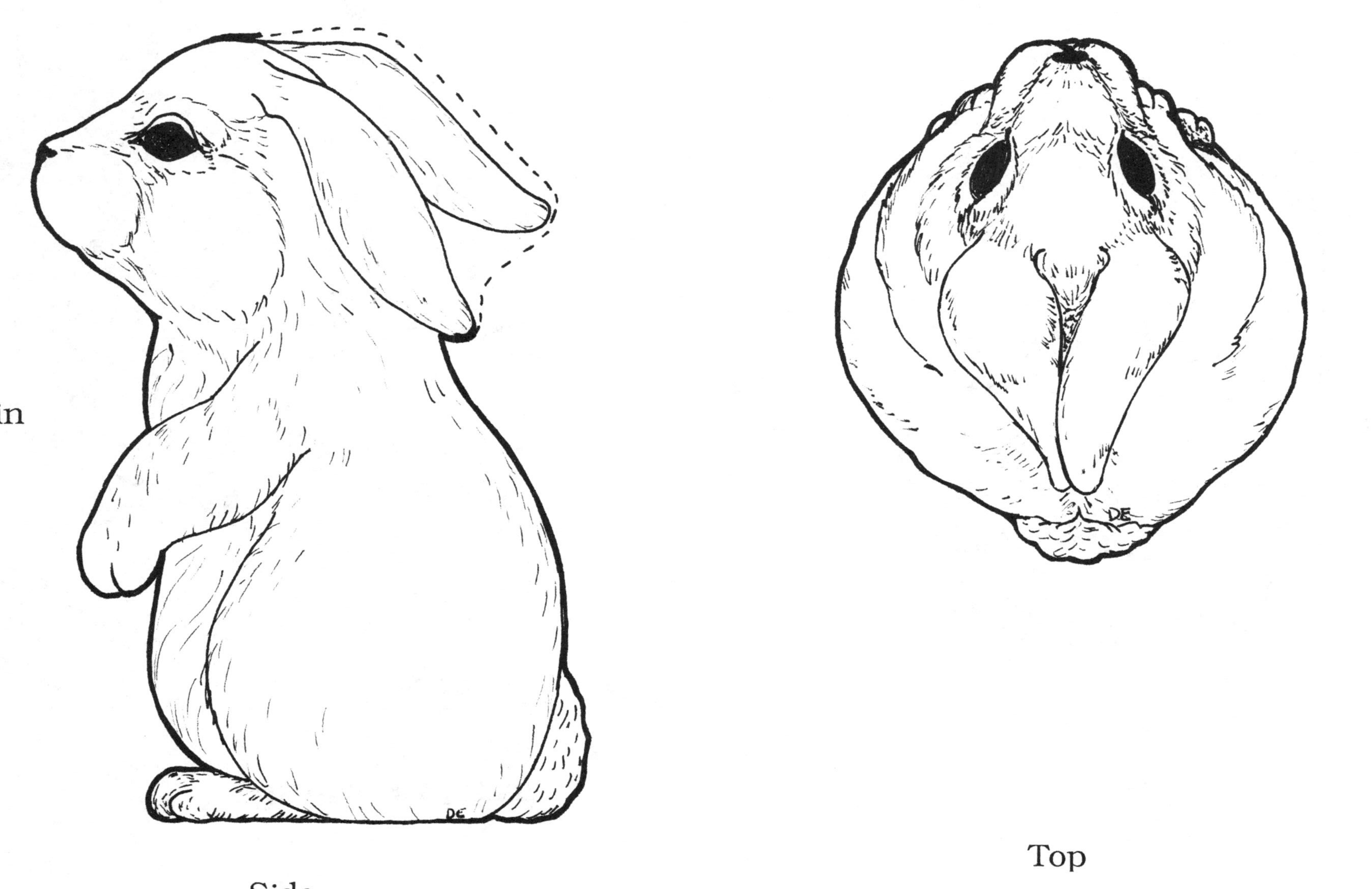

Bunny Pattern

Napping Bunny

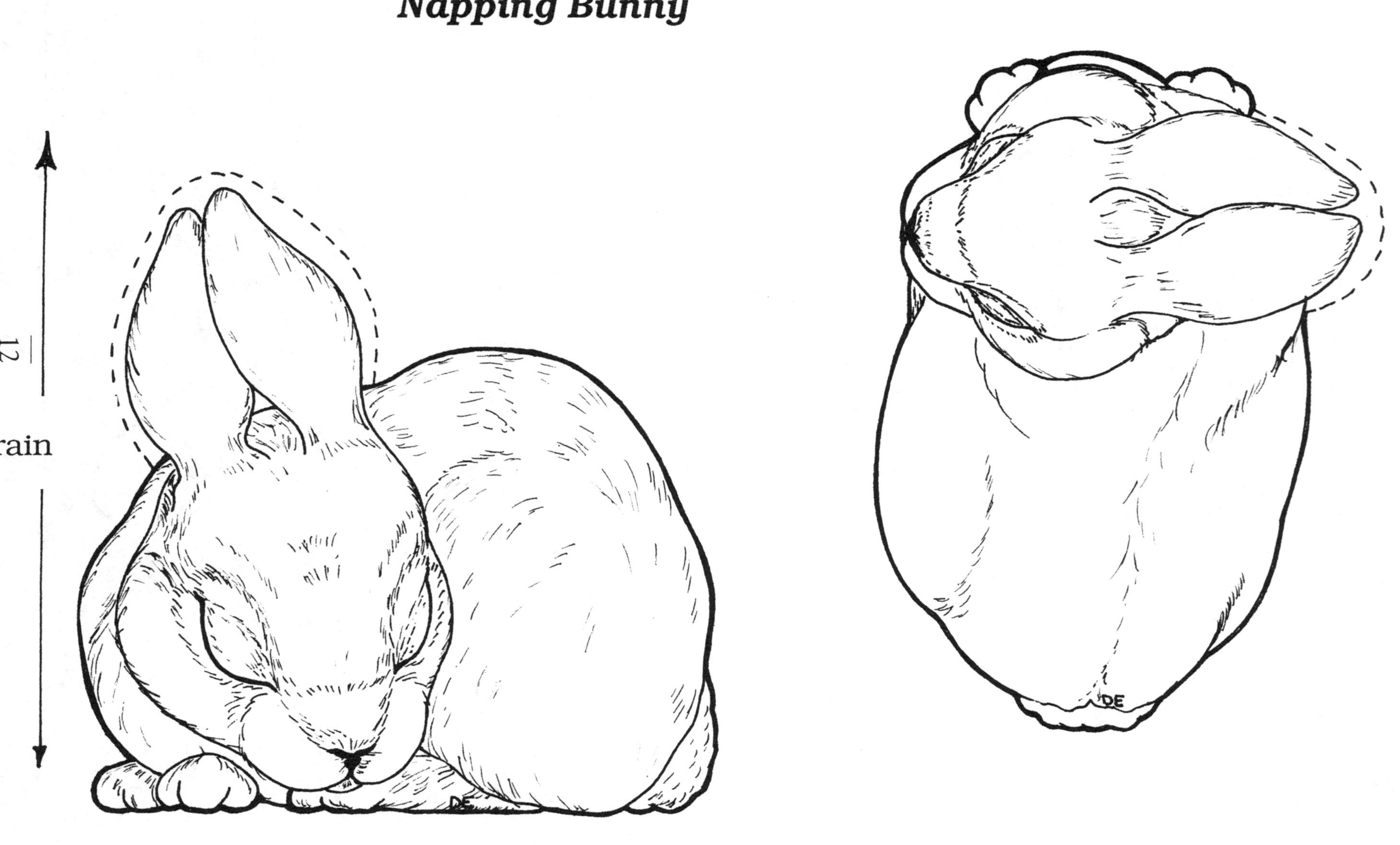

Bunny Pattern

Napping Bunny

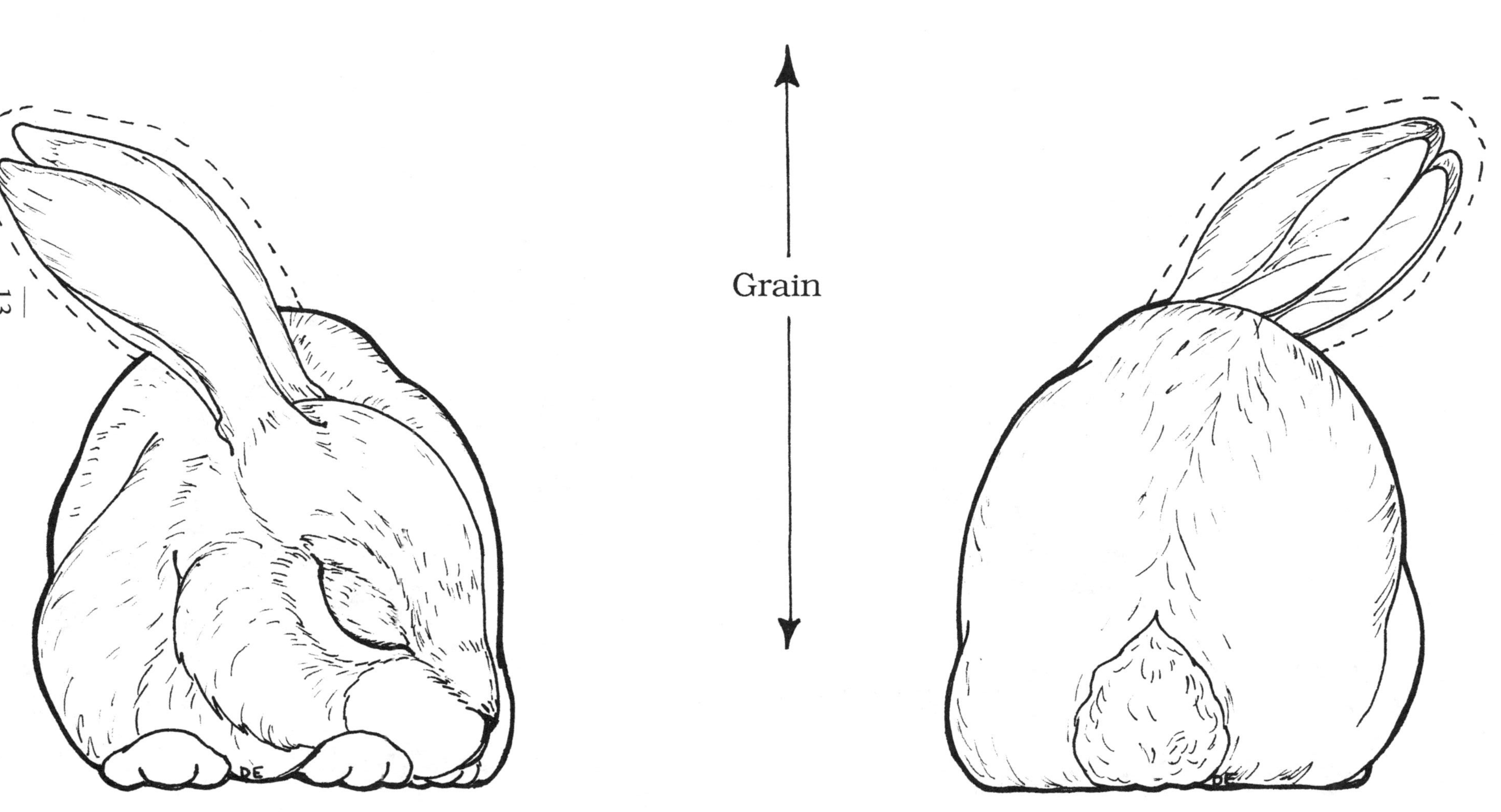

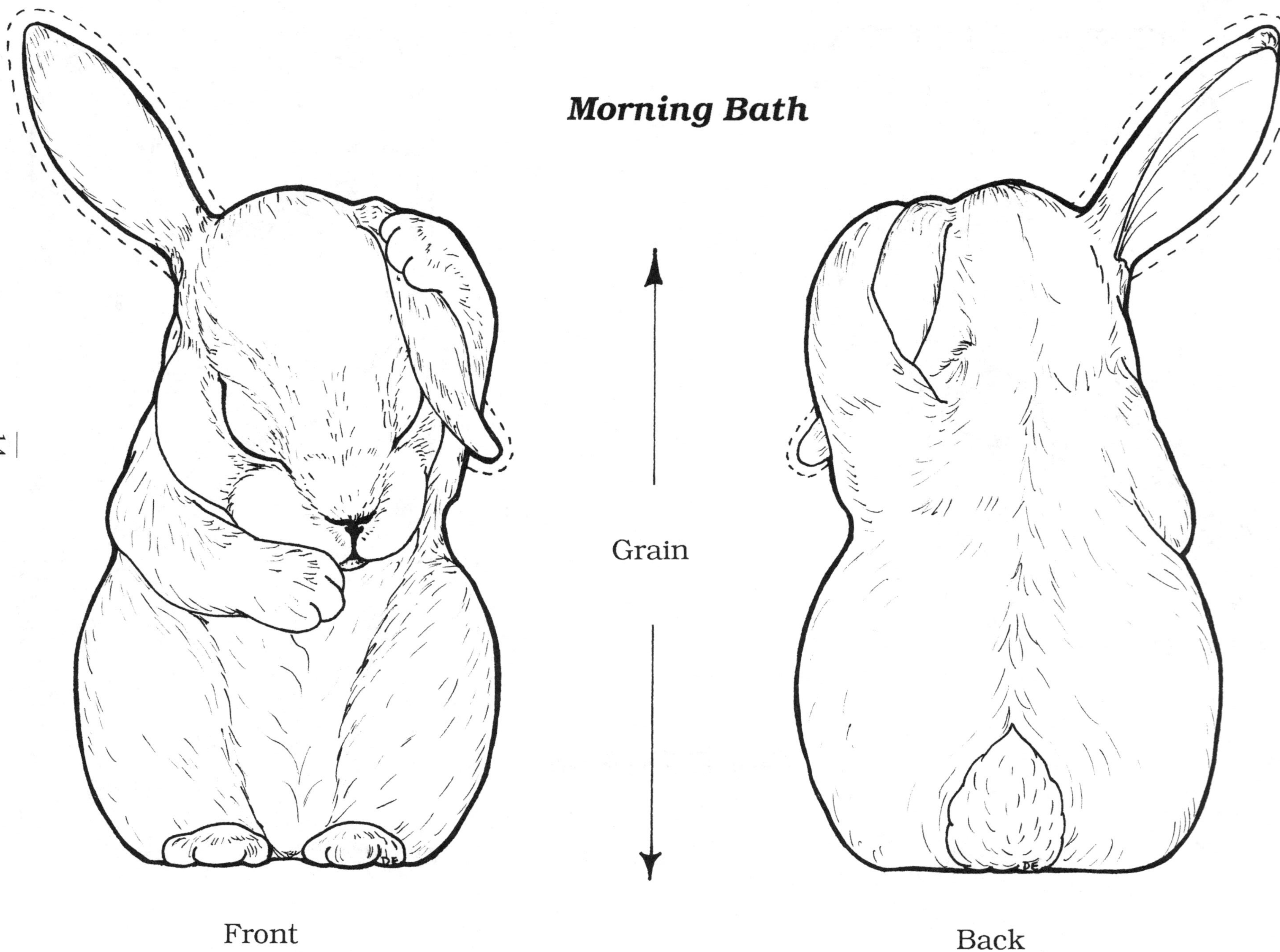

Morning Bath
Grain
Front
Back

Bunny Pattern

Morning Bath

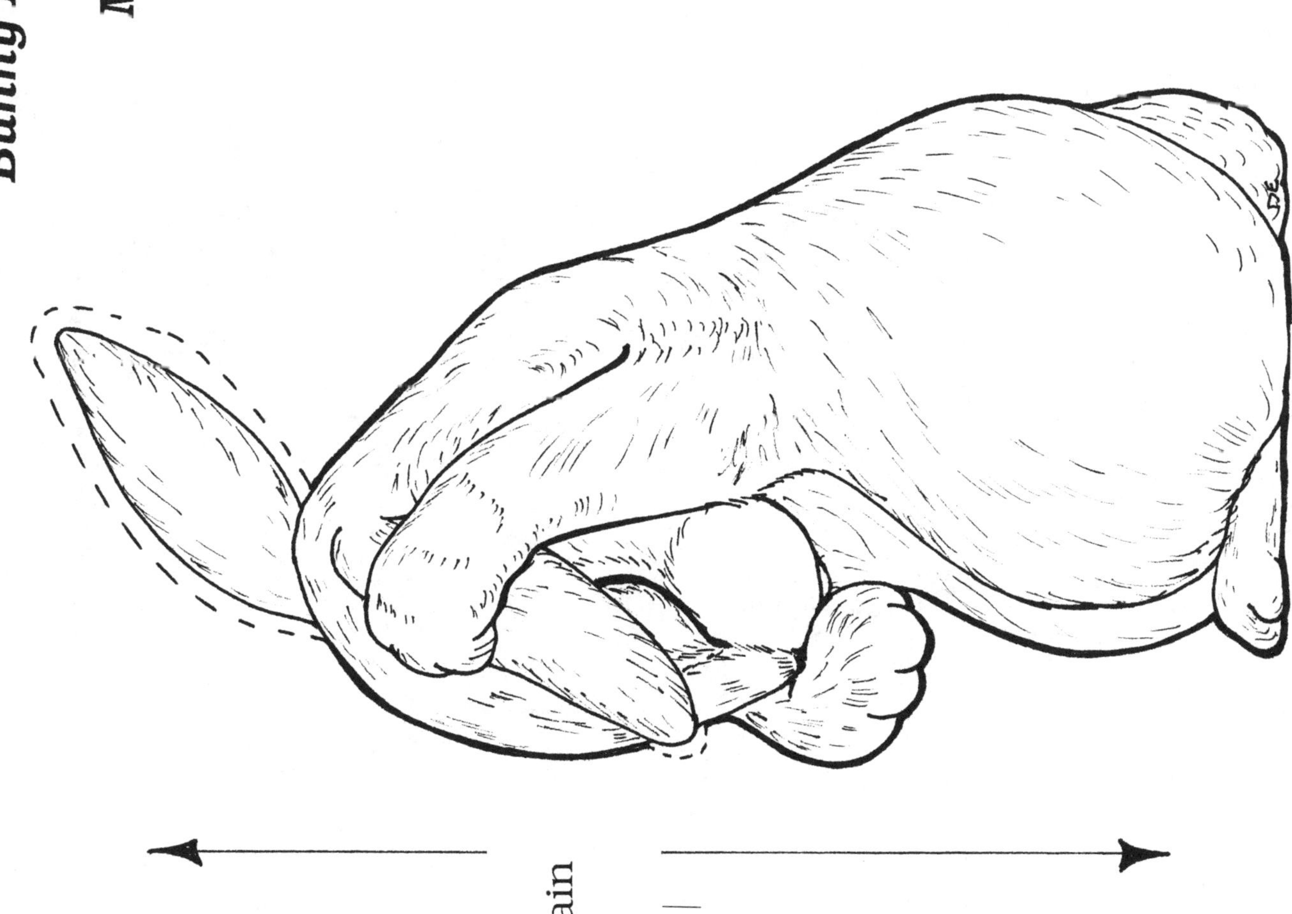

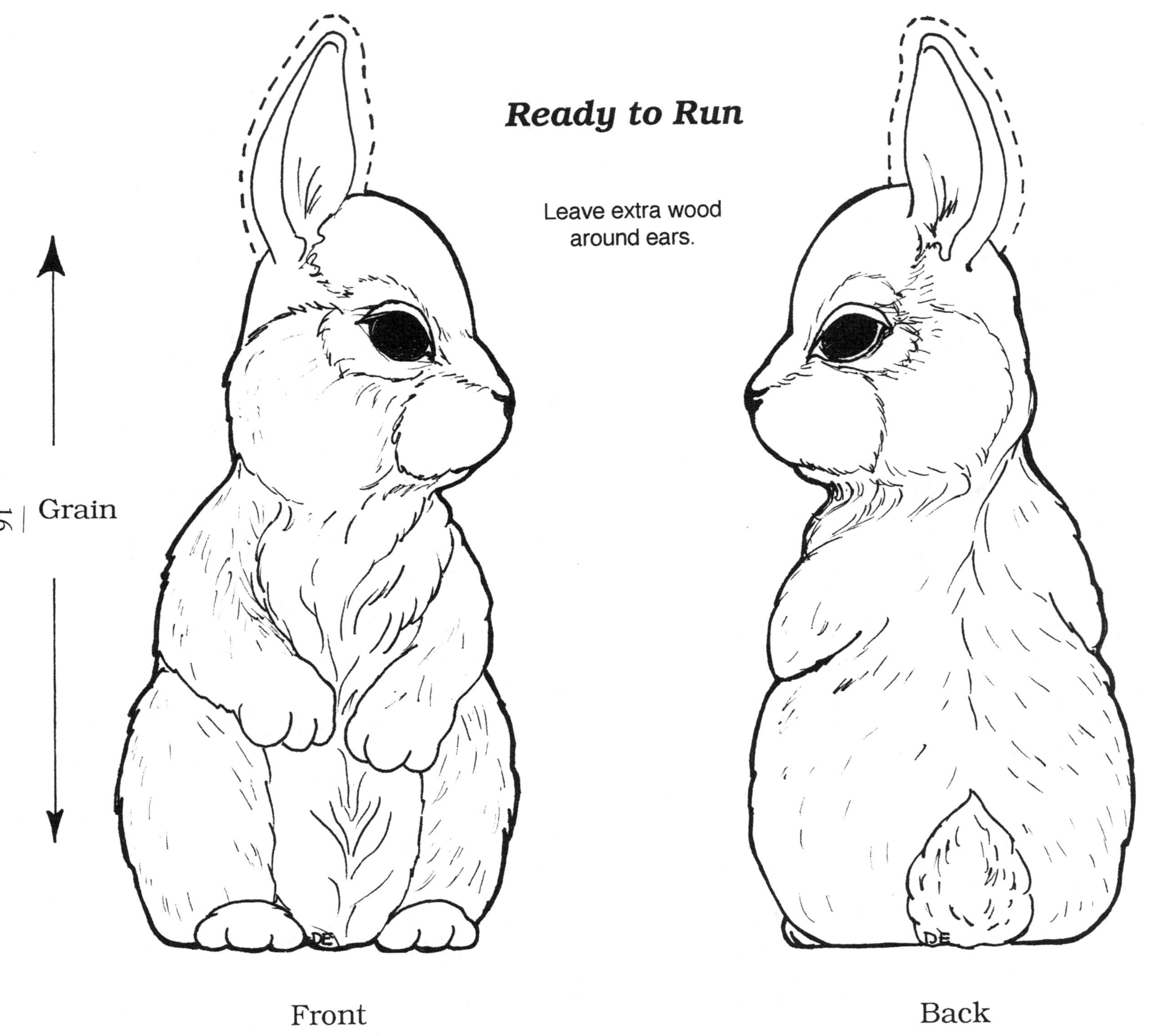

Ready to Run
Leave extra wood
around ears.
Grain
16
Front
Back

Ready to Run

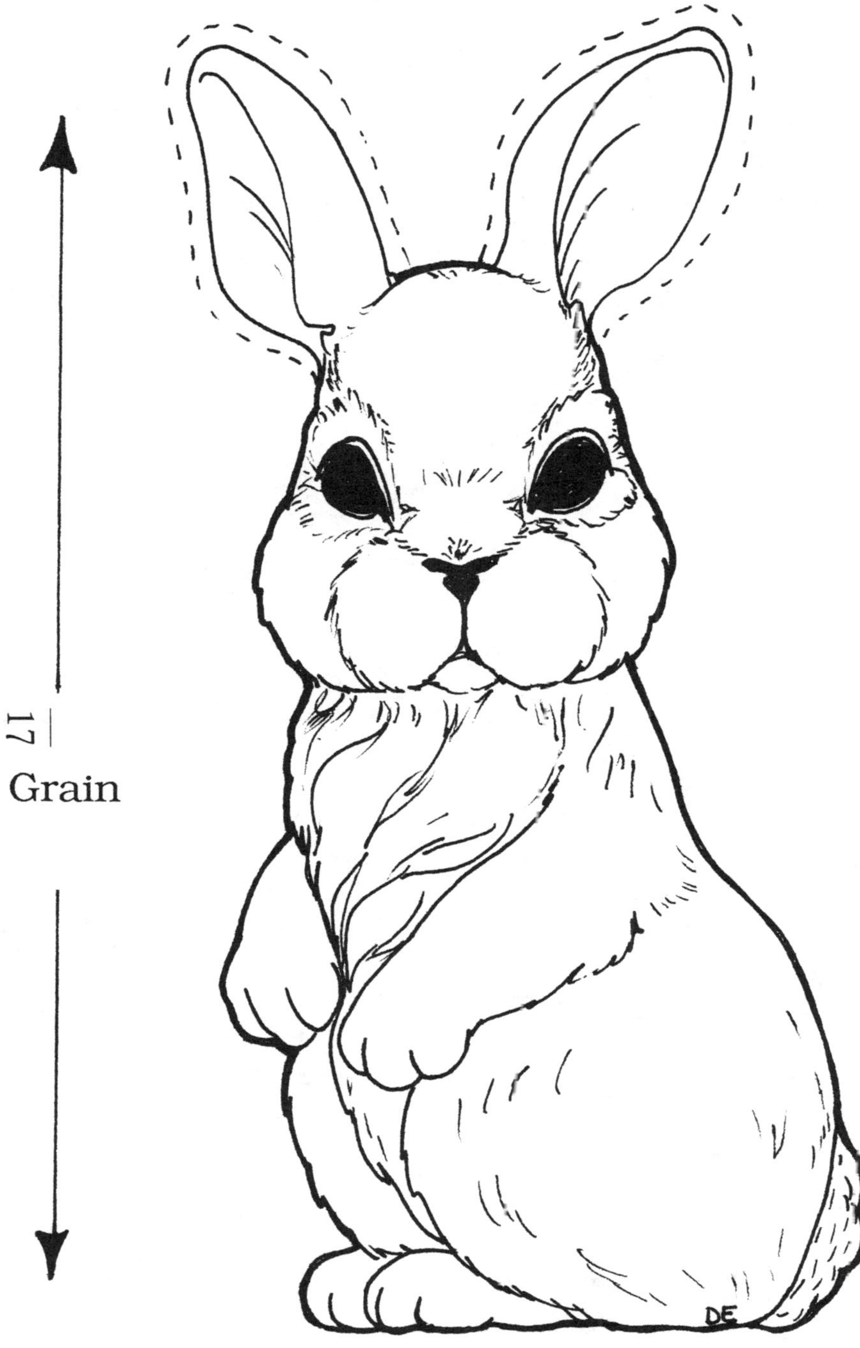

Freeze!

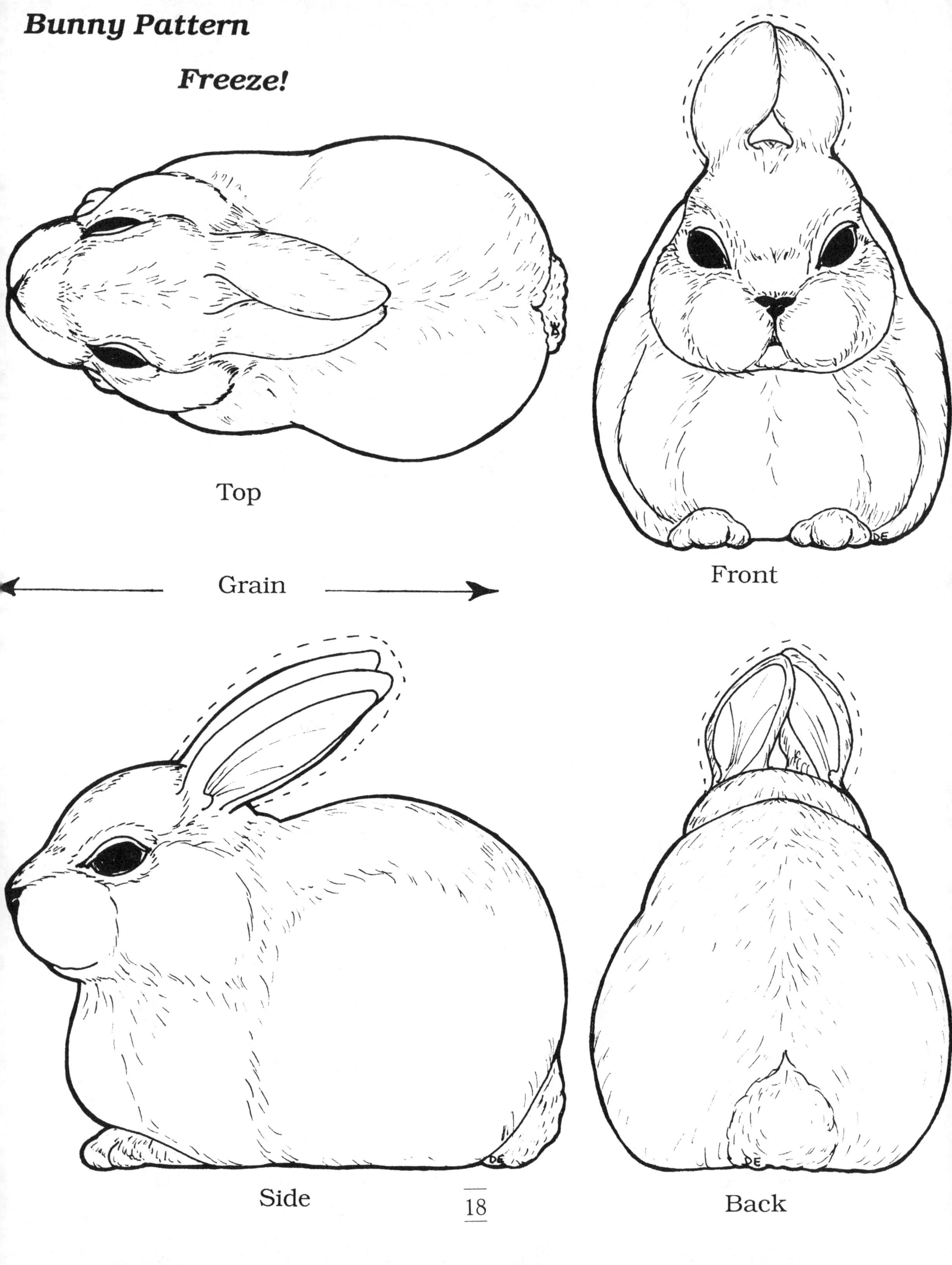

Puppy Pattern

Sloppy Kisser

Front

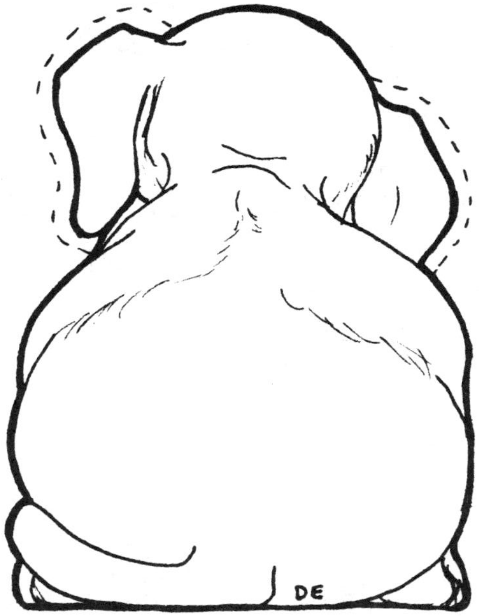

Back

Top

Side

Grain

19

Jr. Watch Dog

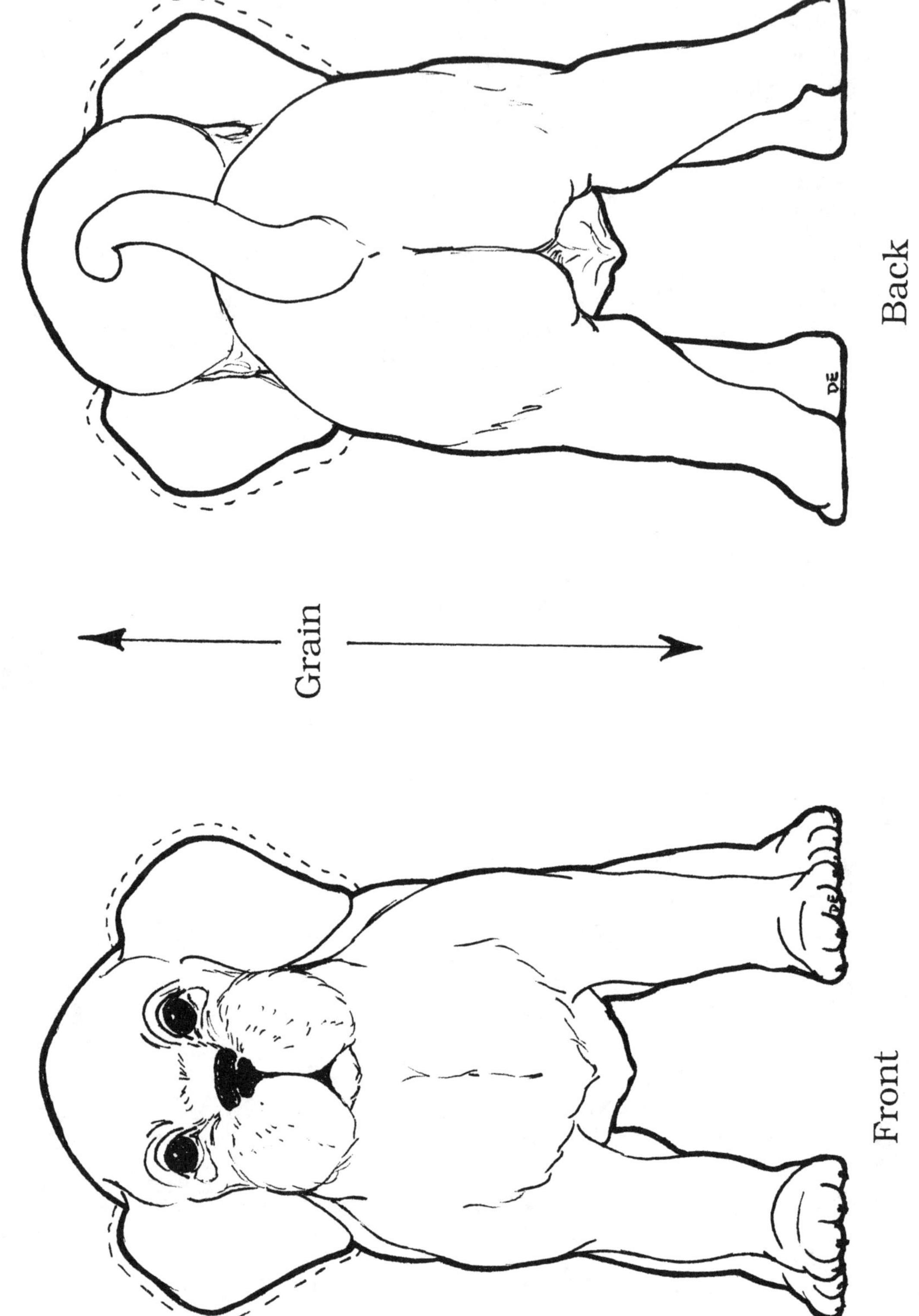

Puppy Pattern

Jr. Watch Dog

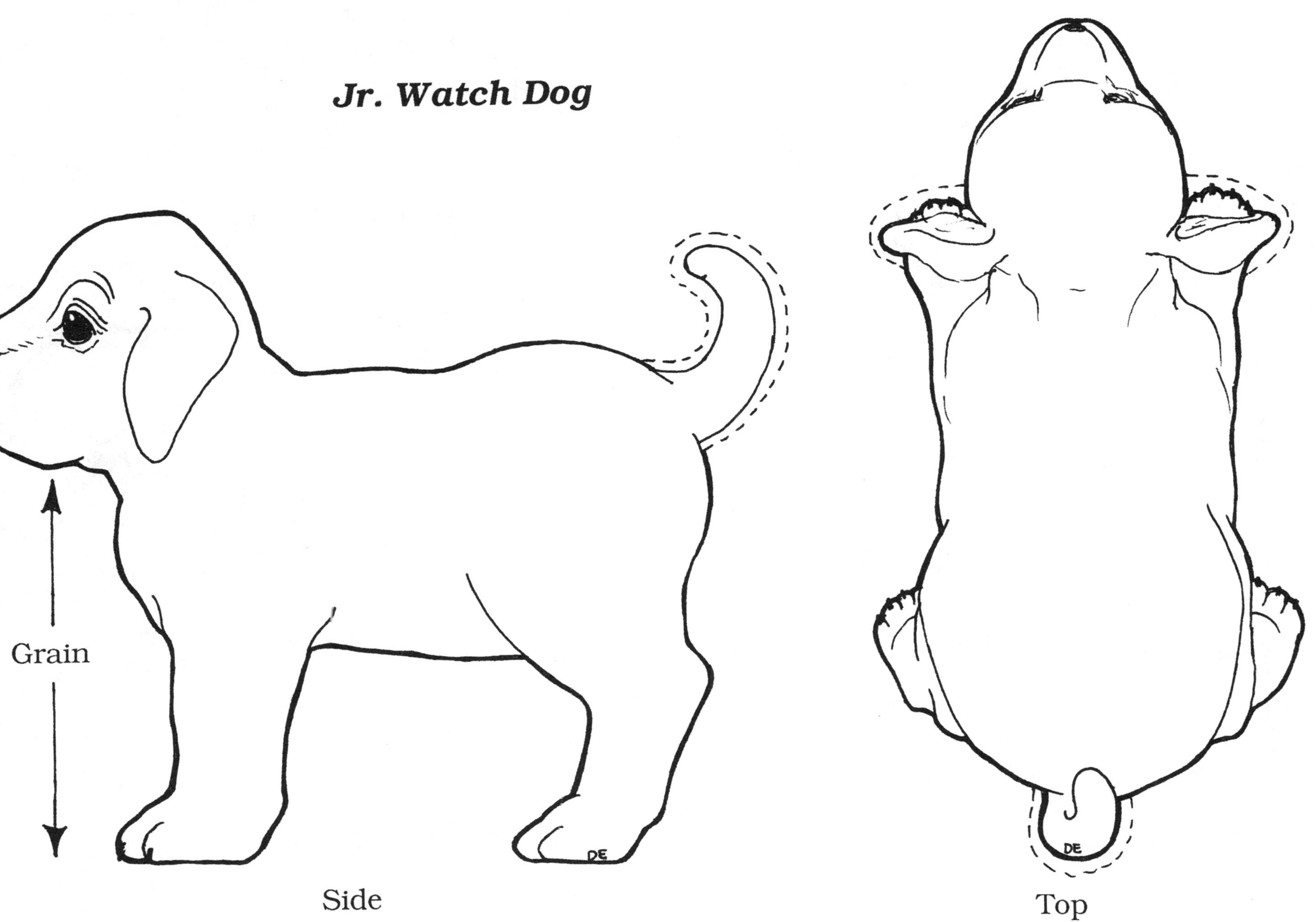

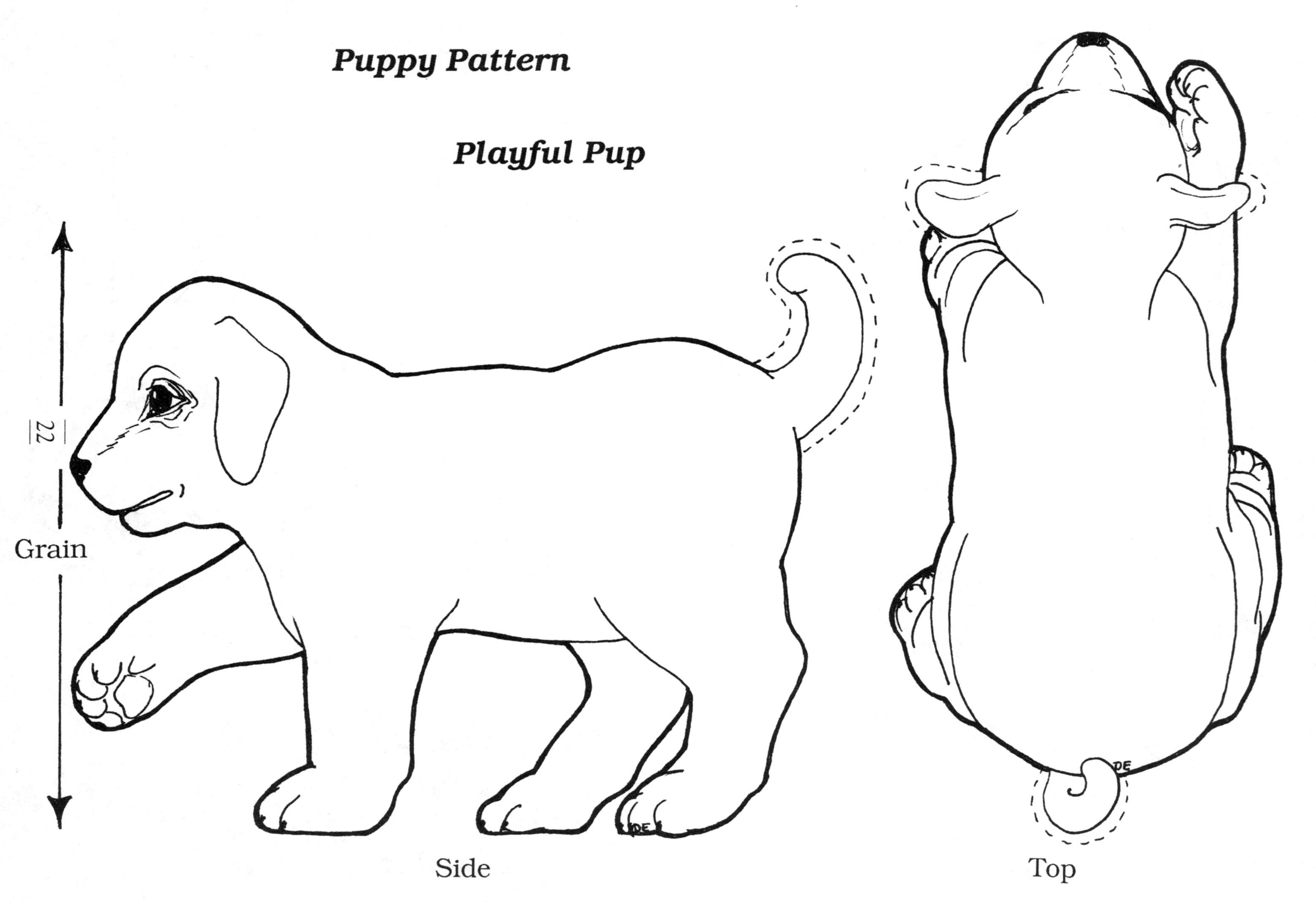

Puppy Pattern
Playful Pup
22
Grain
Side
Top

Puppy Pattern

Playful Pup

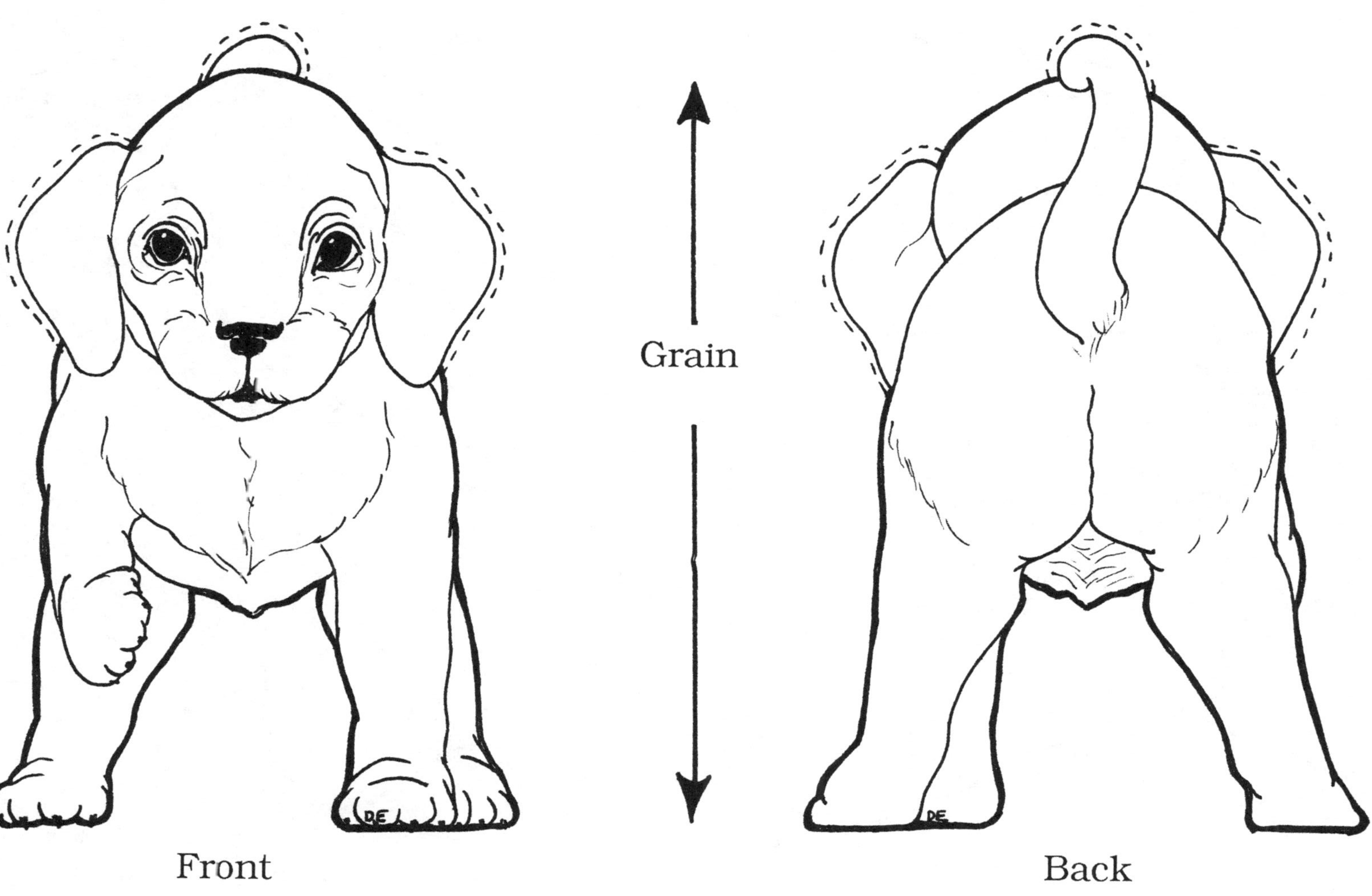

Puppy Pattern

Rainy Day Puppy

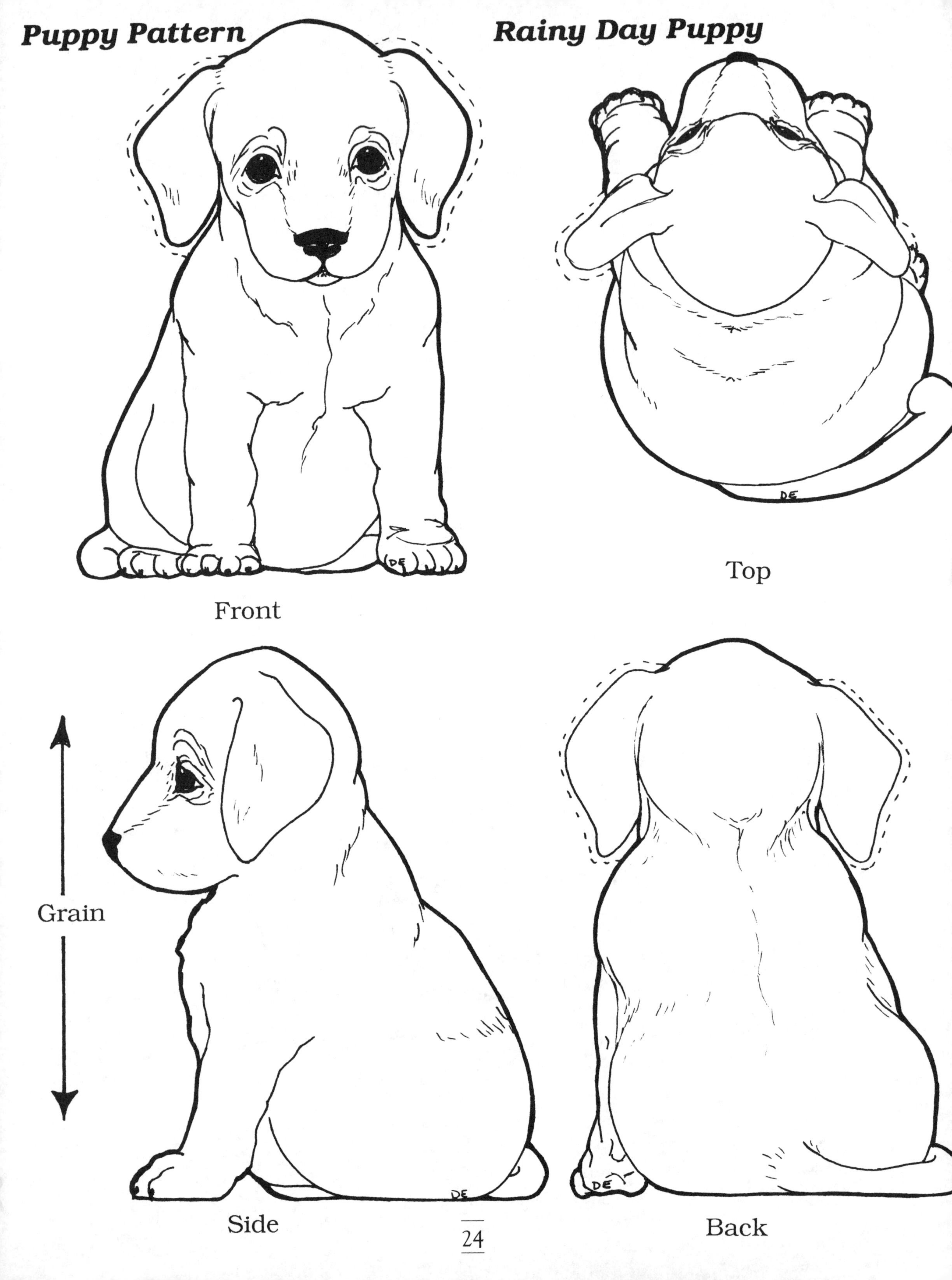

Puppy Pattern

Howler

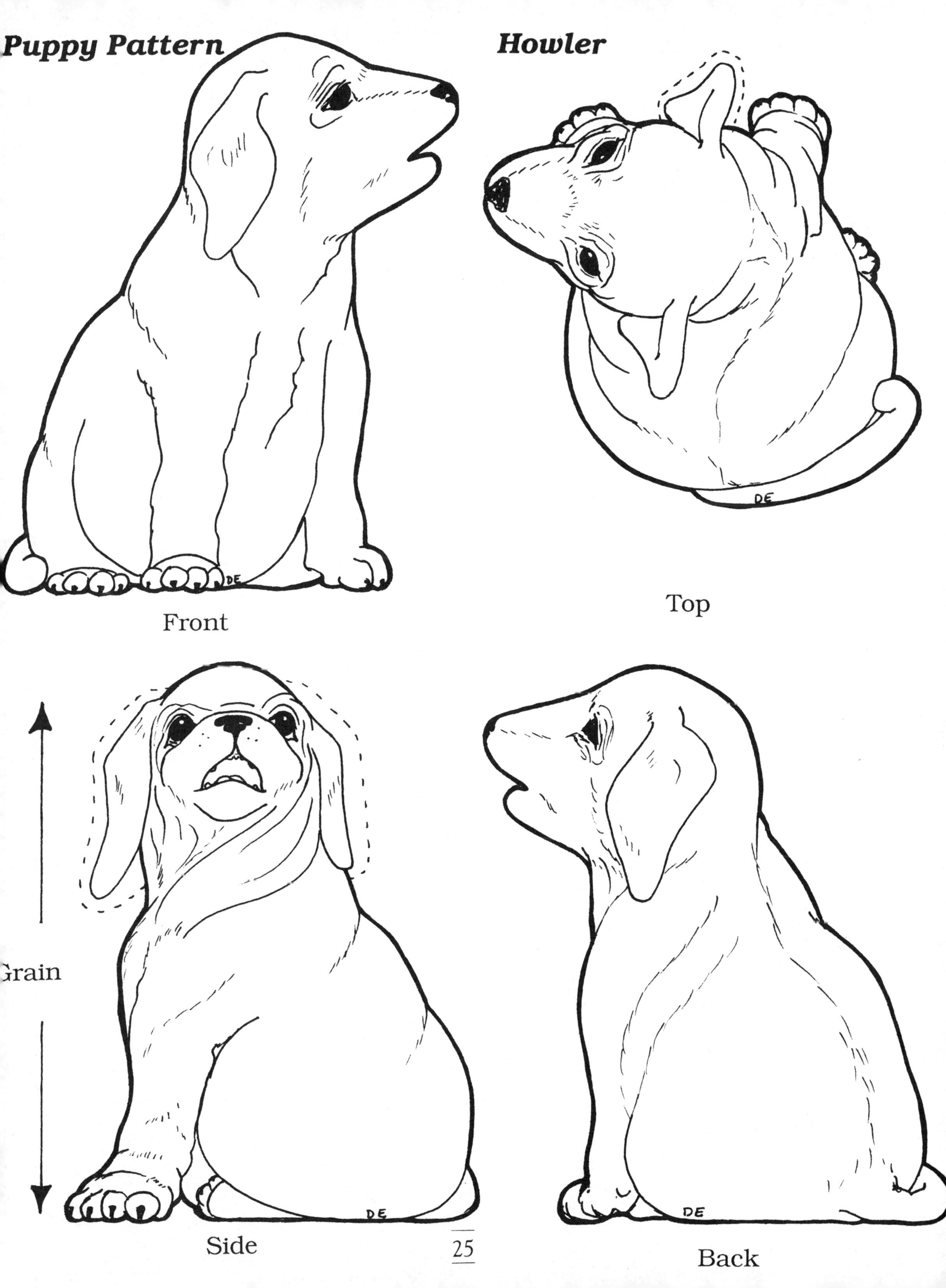

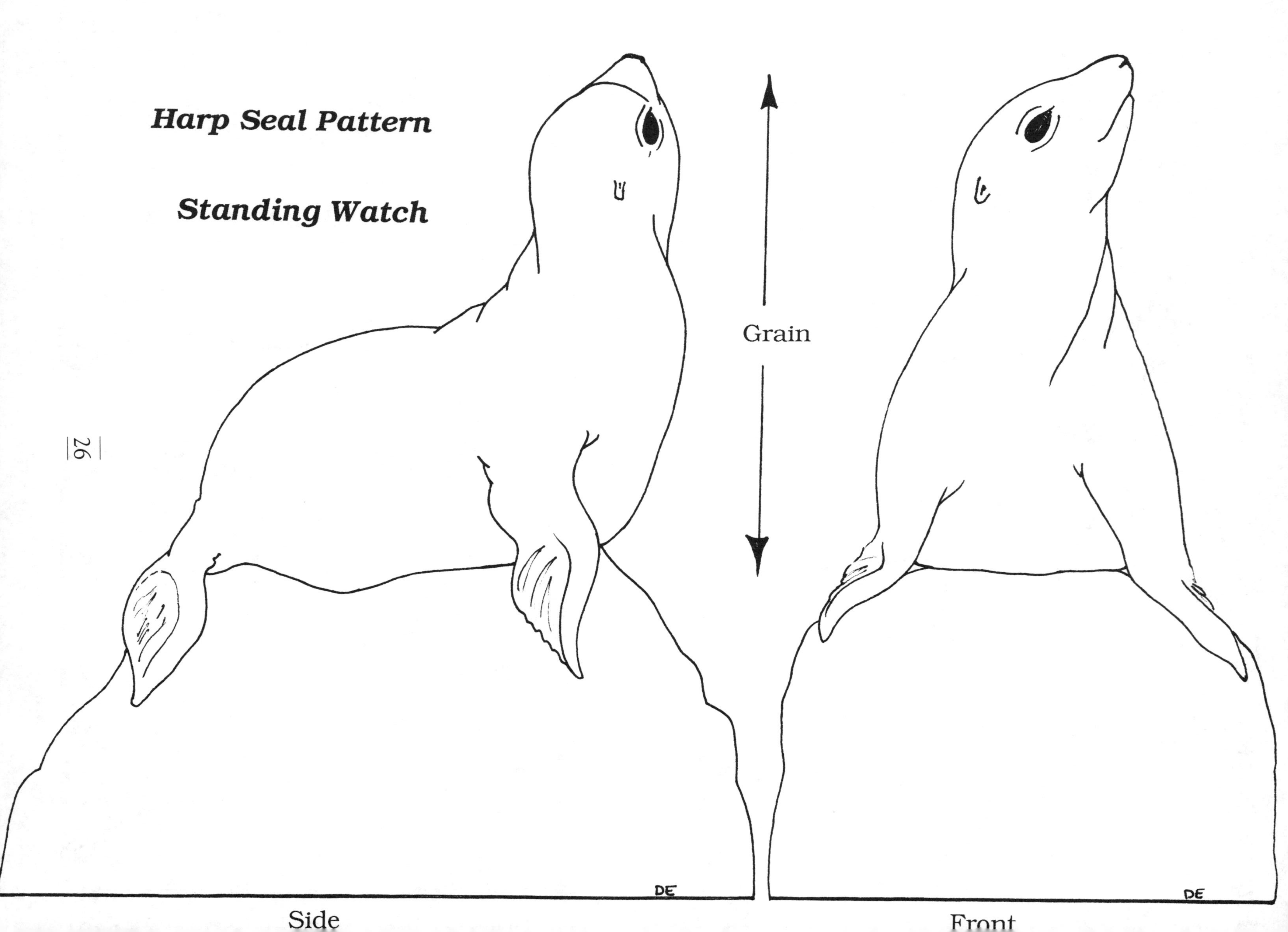

Harp Seal Pattern
Standing Watch
Grain
Side
Front
26

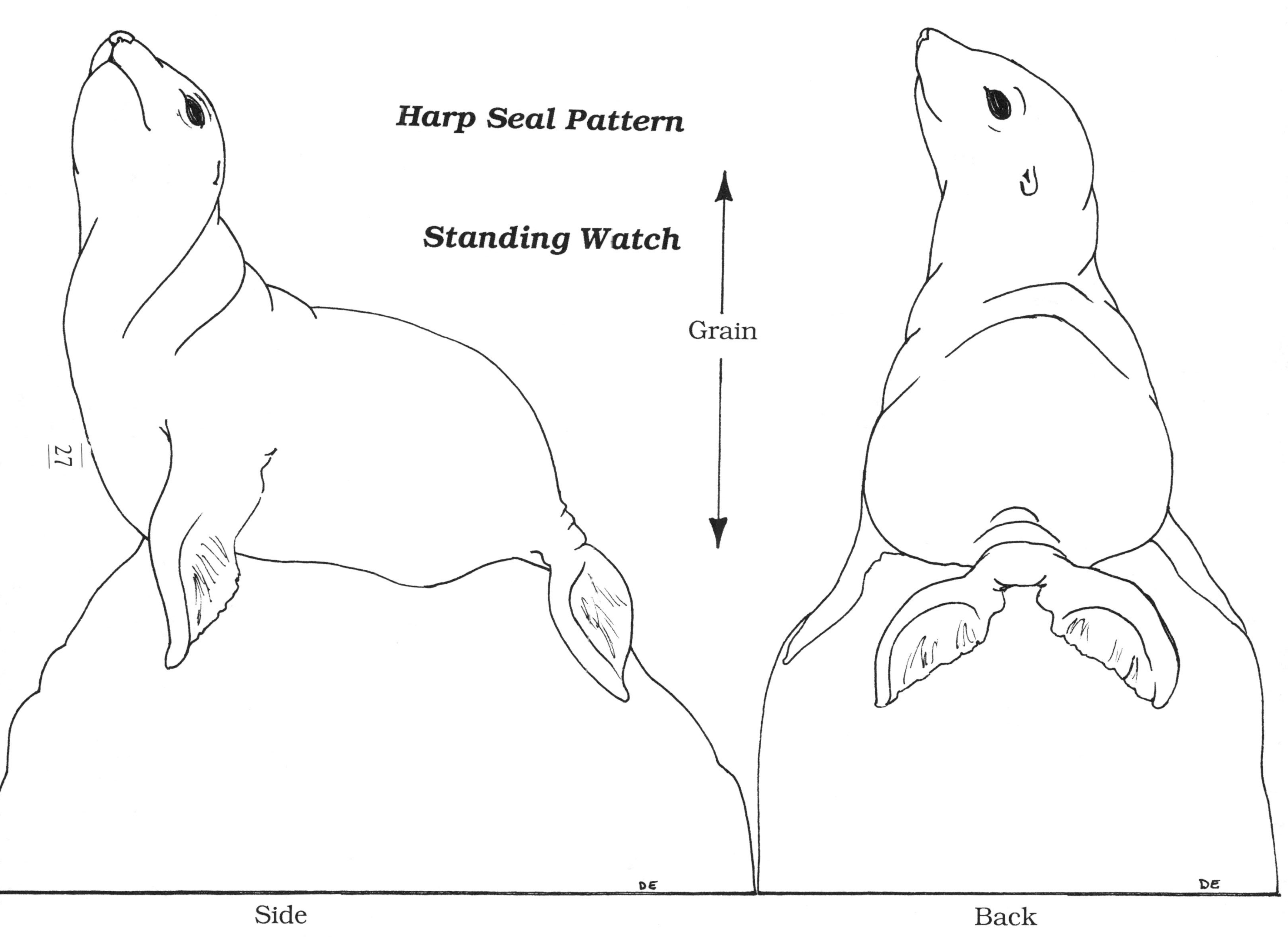

Harp Seal Pattern
Standing Watch
Grain
27
DE
DE
Side
Back

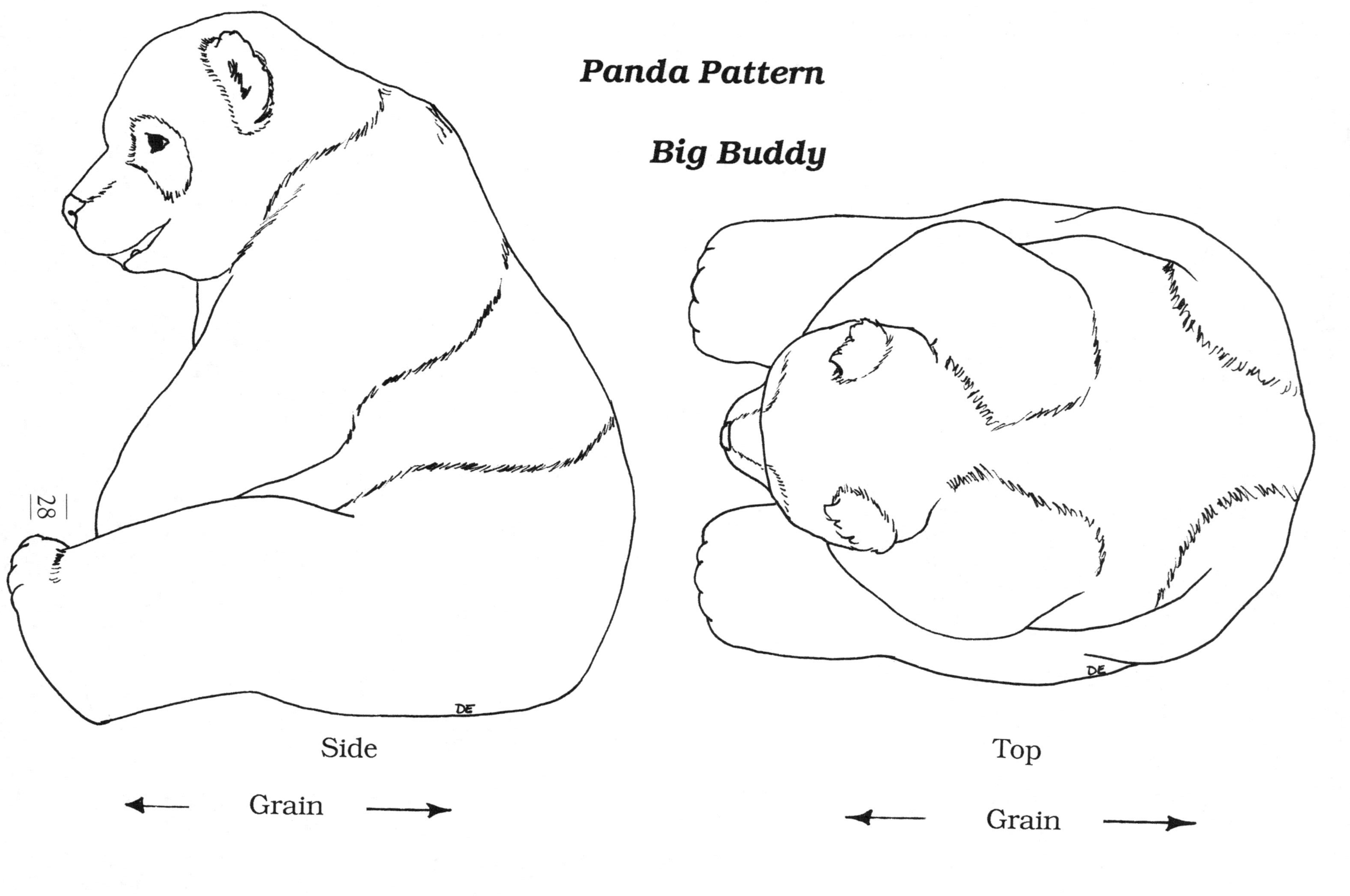

Panda Pattern
Big Buddy
Side
Grain
Top
Grain
28

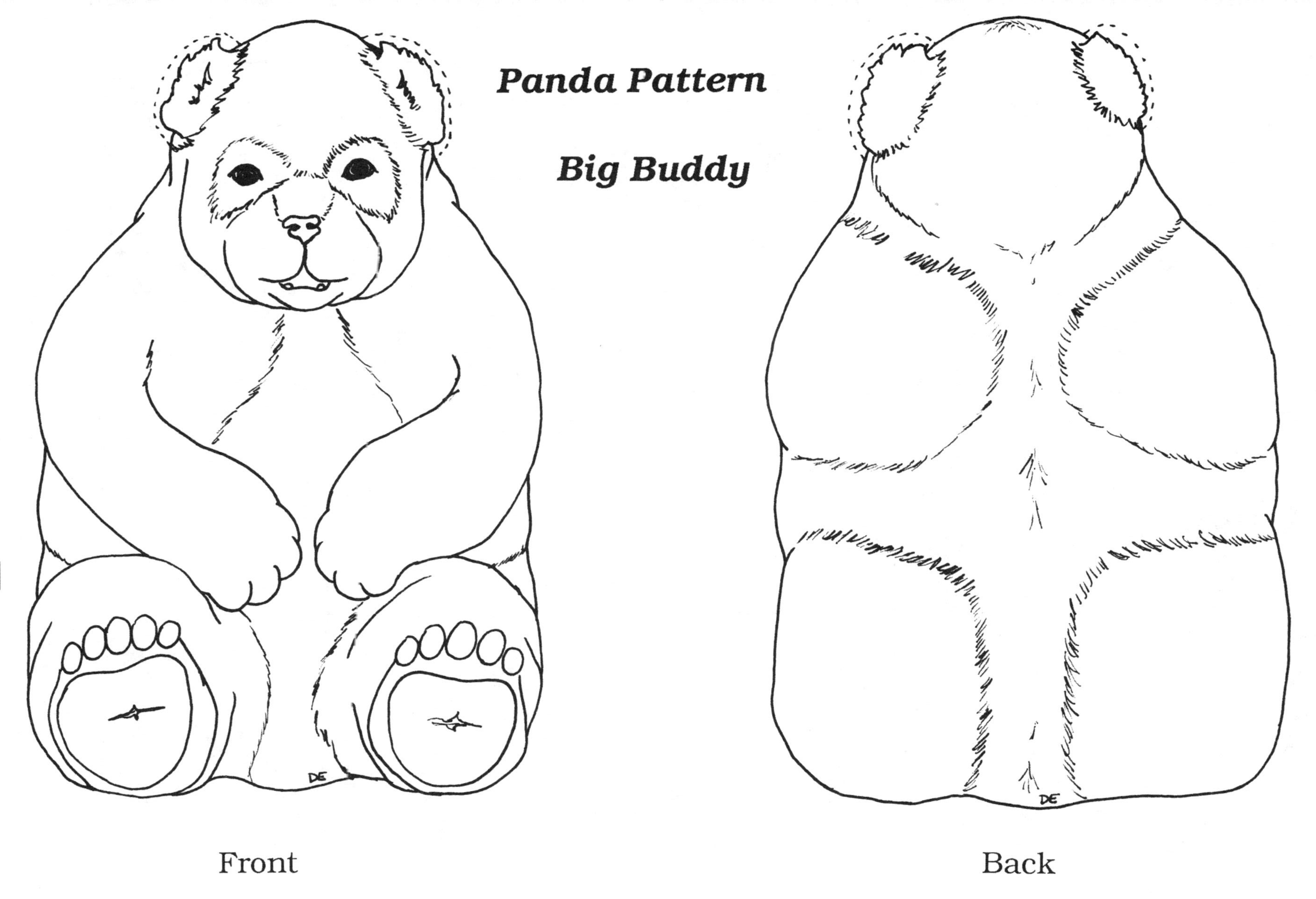

Panda Pattern
Big Buddy
Front
Back

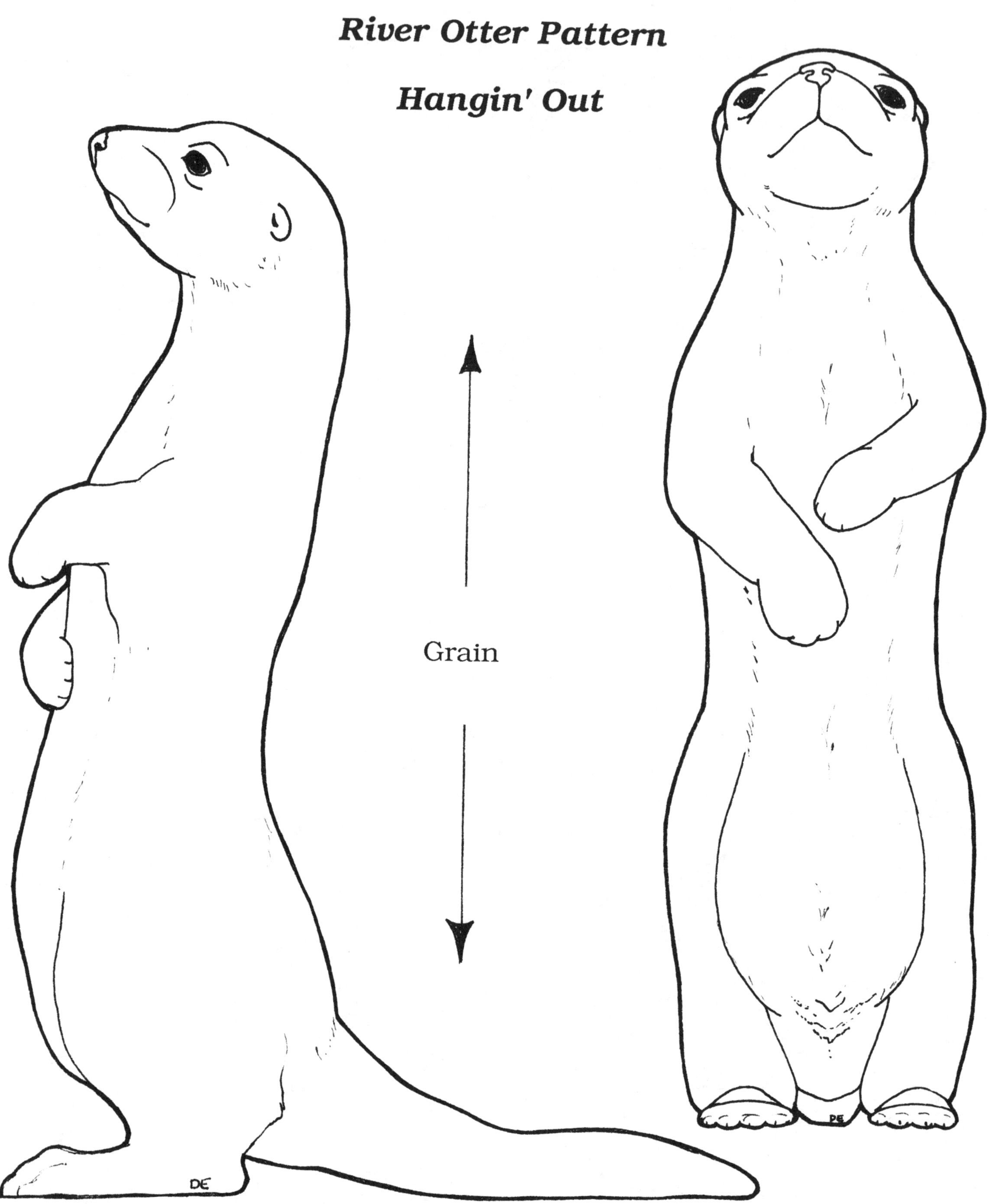

River Otter Pattern

Hangin' Out

Grain

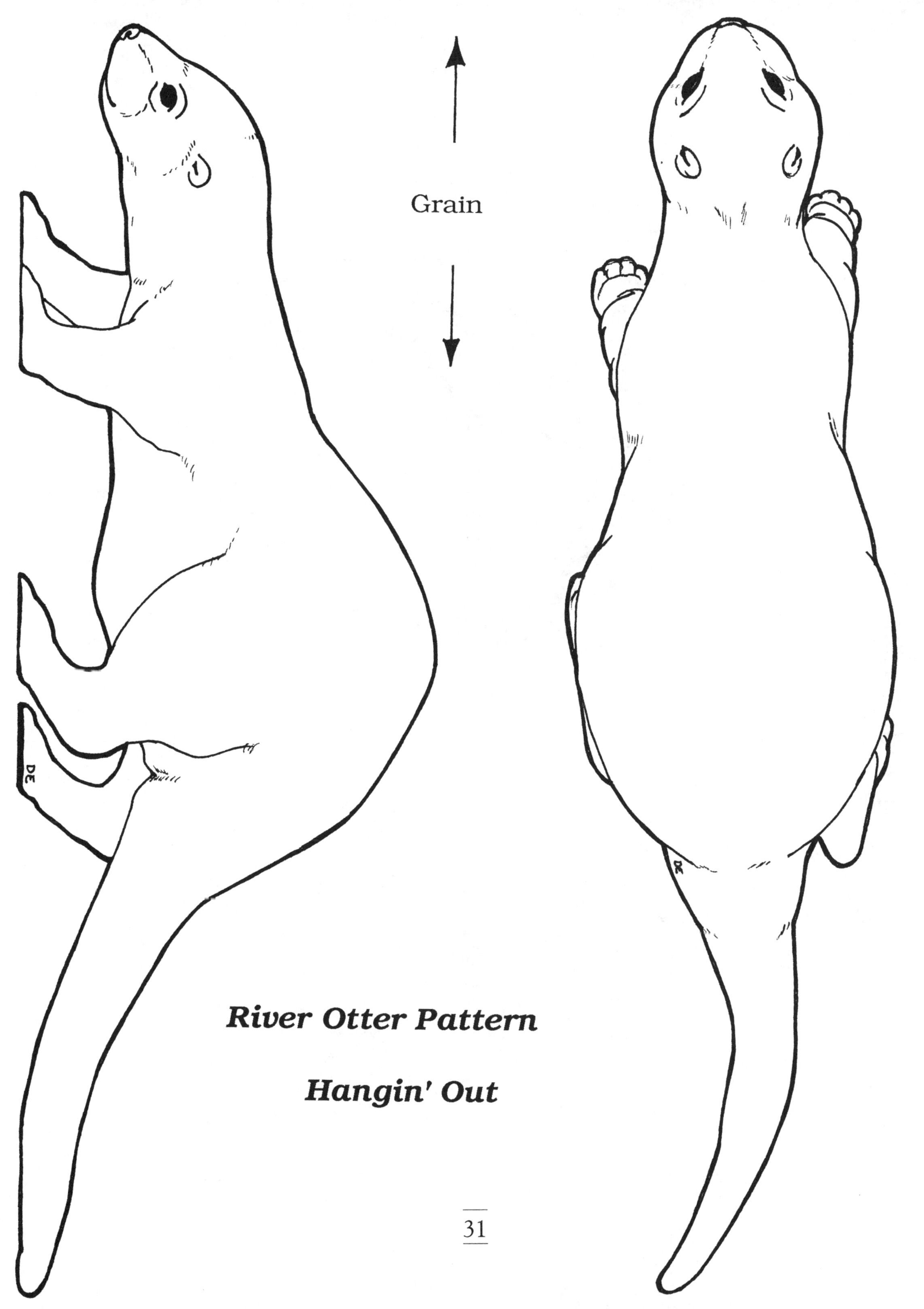

River Otter Pattern

Hangin' Out

Chipmunk Pattern

Having a Bite

Front

Side

Chipmunk Pattern

Sitting Pretty

Side

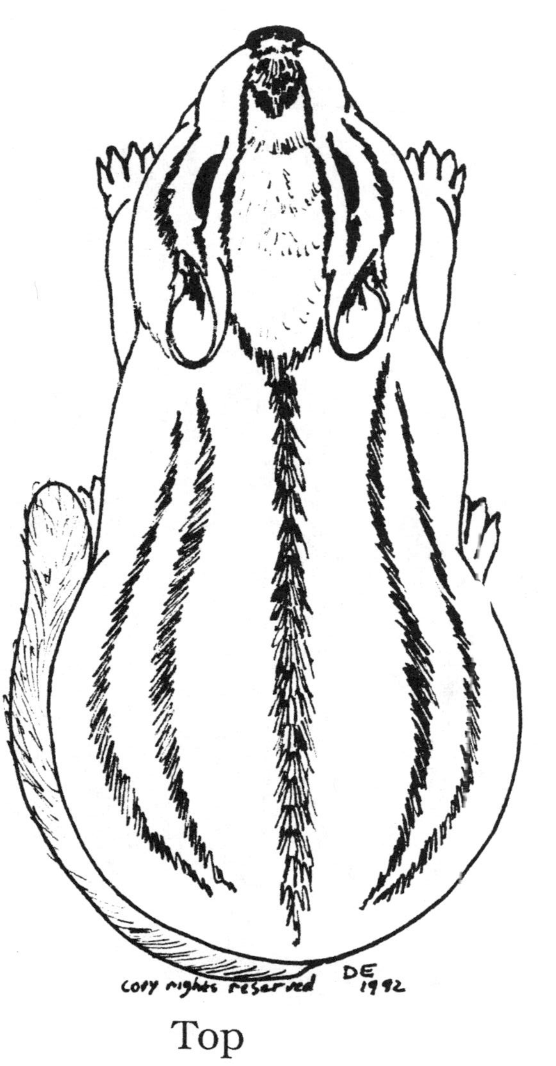

Top

Two tail positions shown.

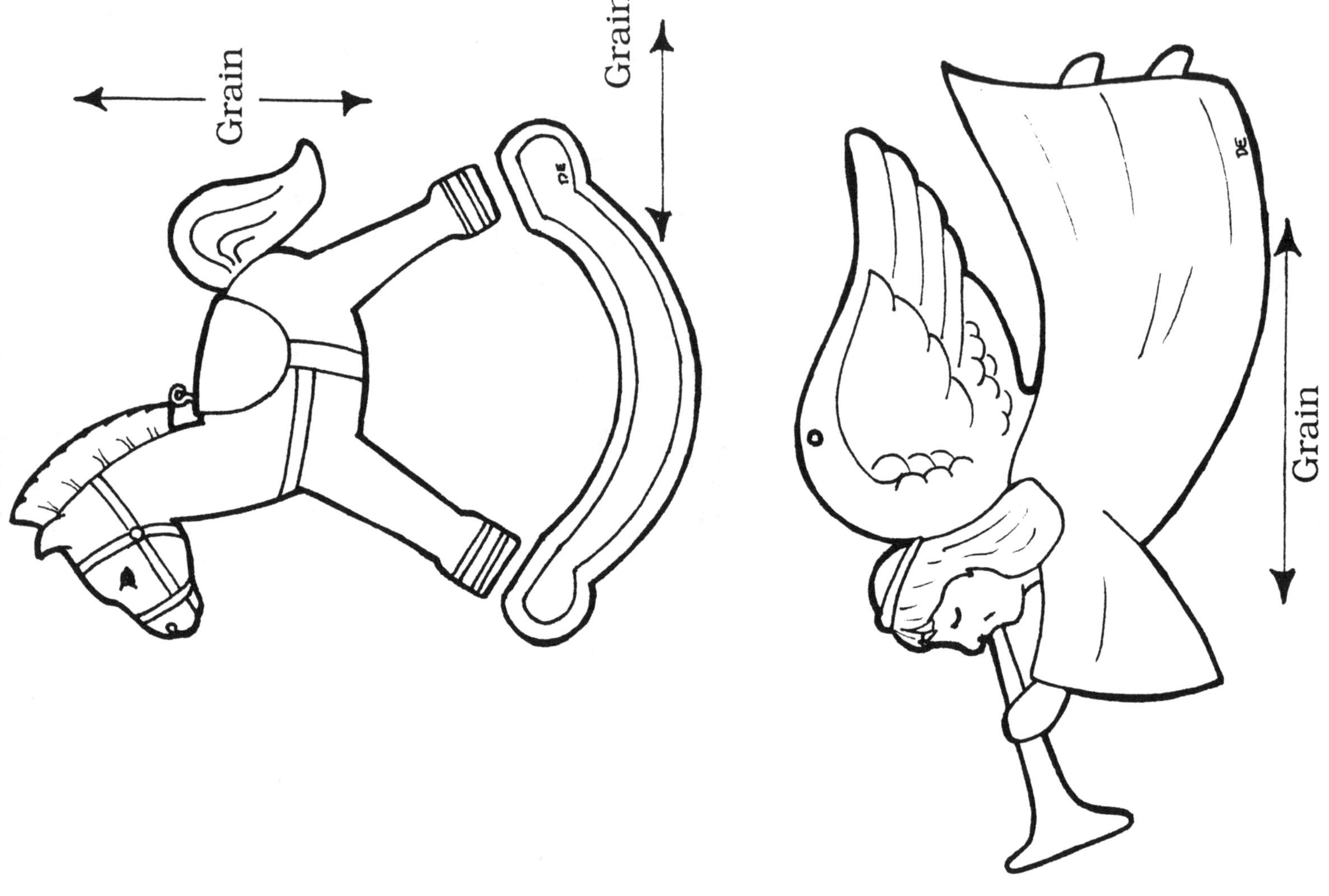

Holiday Ornaments

Cut from 1" wide stock.

Information for Carvers

Suppliers

There are many reputable carving tool suppliers across the country. Below I have listed the ones that I have had experience in dealing with.

An excellent source for information on carving information, shows, clubs and suppliers is the National Wood Carvers' Association. They publish an excellent magazine, "Chip Chats," which every carver should have. (See information on the NWCA in the back of this book.)

Beaver Dam Decoys & Carving Supplies
3311 State Route 305, P.O. Box 40
Cortland, OH 44410
(216) 637-4007

Ritter Carvers
1559 Dillon Road
Maple Glen, PA 19002
(215) 646-4896

Books Plus
42 Charles Street
Lodi, NJ 07644
(201) 478-1144
(201) 478-6022

Foredom Tool Company
16 Stoney Hill Road
Bethel, CT 06801
(203) 792-8622

You are invited to Join the
National Wood Carvers Association
"Some carve their careers: others just chisel"
since 1953

If you have any interest in woodcarving: if you carve wood, create wood sculpture or even just whittle in your spare time, you will enjoy your membership in the National Wood Carvers Association. The non-profit NWCA is the world's largest carving club with over 33,000 members. There are NWCA members in more than 56 countries around the globe.

The Association's goals are to:

- promote wood carving
- foster fellowship among member enthusiasts
- encourage exhibitions and area get togethers
- list sources of equipment and information for the wood carving artist
- provide a forum for carving artists

The NWCA serves as a valuable network of tips, hints and helpful information for the wood carver. Membership is only $11.00 per year.

Members receive the magazine "Chip Chats" six times a year, free with their membership. "Chip Chats" contains articles, news events, demonstrations of technique, patterns and a full color section showcasing examples of fine craftsmanship. Through this magazine you will be kept up to date on shows and workshops to attend, new products, special offers to NWCA members and other members' activities in your area and around the world.

National Wood Carvers Association
7424 Miami Ave.
Cincinnati, OH 45243

Name: ____

Address: ____

____

Dues $11.00 per year in USA, $14.00 per year foreign (payable in US Funds)